LONESOME
monsters

by

Bud
OSBORN

Anvil Press Publishers

VANCOUVER/CANADA

Anvil Press Publishers
PO Box 3008, Station Terminal
Vancouver, B.C. V6B 3X5
CANADA

All Rights Reserved

No part of this book may be reproduced in any form or by any means, electronic or mechanical, without permission in writing from the publisher, except by a reviewer, who may quote brief passages in a review to print in a magazine or newspaper or to be broadcast on radio or television.

Resemblances to people alive or dead are purely intentional.

© Bud Osborn, 1995

2nd Printing: September 2023

CANADIAN CATALOGUING IN PUBLICATION DATA

Osborn, Walton (Bud)

Lonesome monsters
Poems.
ISBN 1-895636-08-6
I. Title.
PS8579.S33L66 1995 C811'.54 C95-910384-8
PR9199.3.082L66 1995

SOME OF THESE POEMS APPEARED PREVIOUSLY IN THE FOLLOWING JOURNALS & ANTHOLOGIES:
Phoenix Rising, Inkstone, Semiotext[e] USA, The Minnesota Review, sub-TERRAIN Magazine, Bouillabaisse, Grain, Event, Carnegie Newsletter and in two anthologies: East of Main and Downtown Eastside Poets.

CONTENTS

mission news / 7
mullin's brother / 8
when I was 15 / 9
keys to kingdoms / 14
for kids who kill themselves because of braces / 23
refuge / 25
drapetomania / 26
new home / 27
dreams in the americas / 28
guilty as charged / 30
historical site / 33
4 haiku / 34
love poem / 35
hank / 37
lonesome monsters / 40
reparation / 41
after the strike / 42
drifting / 44
one year to the next / 50
social services / 52
reality for rent / 53
getting culture / 55
propaganda / 57
3 haiku / 60
houses of the dying / 61

probably / 64
outside this hotel a man is freezing to death / 66
promenade park past midnight / 67
demolition derby / 68
a found poem of lucy b. / 69
down here / 70
zoned residential / 78
no wonder I can't solve my problems / 80
Killing Yourself and Living Through It / 81
street theatre / 86
community life / 88
3 haiku / 90
something's going around / 91
Hounded to the Coast / 98

this book is dedicated to

jack micheline, whose example has inspired me

cuba marie dyer, whose faith has strengthened me

leslie ottavi, whose love has sustained me

the primary intention in my writing has been fidelity to the experiences of the people about whom i write.

— B.O.

**the word "monster"
derives from the latin root "monere"
which means "to warn"**

---

mission news

it's early about 40 minutes before they're
supposed to let us in & some people wait on
the sidewalk & roll cigarettes & others lay
down in the weeds across the street & a few
stick their faces in paper sacks & sniff
glue but most stand by the fence waiting for
someone inside to take the german shepherd
off its long chain so we can line up by the
door but one guy crosses the asphalt & the
dog jumps up barking like a madman & pulls
at its chain & the guy shuffles closer to it
inches at a time & someone yells "leave the
dog alone!" but the guy keeps going & some-
body shouts "get away from it for chrissake!"
& the dog's frantic its fur sticking straight
up & the guy edges nearer & the dog's on its
hind legs & lunges & would've ripped the guy's
throat open if he hadn't turned his back &
swung his arm instead into the shepherd's
jaws & the guy screams & we make noise & a
mission worker comes outside & calms down
the dog & then an old man says "he was lucky,
dog coulda ate his ass!" & we laugh glad to
laugh at anything standing there shifting
weight from one leg to the other

        watching blood dripping
        waiting in line
        for something to eat

mullin's brother

mullin was another 50-year-old loser living in
a halfway house, but he had something that made
him feel good anyway. he wrote perfectly metrical
sonnets, hundreds of them, along the lines
of elizabeth barrett browning & considered himself
a poet without peer. one day mullin was with
his brother in the angry sea inn, talking about
his sonnets & his brother said, "what's so hard
about writing poems nobody wants to read?" "you
can't do it," mullin said. "oh yeah?" replied
his brother. "never," said mullin. "I'll write
a poem right now," his brother said & peeled the label off
his beer bottle, borrowed a pen
from mullin, scribbled something, passed it over
& said, "here, a poem!" mullin looked at it,
read it aloud & said, "that's not a poem. no-
body'd buy that." "I will," said a guy sitting
a few stools away. "I'll buy that poem," he said
& handed a dollar bill to mullin's brother, who'd
written

> bottles full
> bottles empty
> dreams

when I was 15

I read a story in a newspaper
about a man who killed himself
by taking aspirins
it was a way out I'd never considered

I bought a couple family-size bottles
& chose a night
when my parents were at home
sitting downstairs in silence
wishing they were elsewhere
with someone else

I was supposed to be doing school work
memorizing lies
I filled my hand with aspirins
& threw them down my throat
but gagged when I tried to swallow

I got some water & took them a few at a time
in a trance I finished the aspirins
& laid down to die
staring at the ceiling

I began shaking
my stomach bucked against the poison
I heard explosions
white lights flashed
& I sank spinning down an abyss
opening wider & blacker beneath & around me
I panicked

I stood up
my legs collapsed
I hurled myself out of the room
staggered across the hallway
& fell down the stairs
into the living room
where they looked up
from the television

my mother rushed towards me
& asked what'd happened
I told her
she screamed "why?"
my stepfather strolled off to get the car
a smile was on his face

in the sterile fluorescent emergency room
a doctor asked me if I wanted to vomit
or have my stomach pumped
"vomit" I said
another doctor rushed in with the lab report
& said it was "almost too late!"
they'd have to pump
so I struggled to swallow tubes through my nose
& after my life was saved
a cop came in
with a gun & a badge & handcuffs

he couldn't even stomach looking at me
shoved his cold blue eyes in a notebook
& asked me why I did it
no

he shot me with the question
boom!
I told him I didn't know why
he didn't believe me

"come on" he said
"people know why they do things, now tell me!"
I started crying
"come on" he said "why'd you do it?"
"I don't know!" I yelled

"all right" he said
"how are your grades?
do you have a girlfriend?
do you play any sports?"

I groaned
& told him my grades were good
my girlfriend was fine
& I played several sports
"what's her name & address?" the cop asked
I told him all that had nothing to do
with any of this

"hey!" he shouted at me
"do you know your mother is out there pacing the halls?
how do you think she feels about this?
how do you think what you did to her makes her feel?"

the cop was shaking & said
"we've got places
for people who don't know why they do things!"
I wondered where & what they might be

I said "well I guess you'll just have to send me there!"
the cop slapped his notebook closed
shook his head
& walked out of the room

I spent the night in the hospital
in the morning a detective came in smiling
& told me I had a record now
that it was against the law "to try to harm yourself"
he said not to worry about it
smiled
& left the room
then a protestant minister came in
closed his eyes
& prayed into the wall
for the sake of my soul

I'd become a criminal & a sinner

I remembered a cheap paperback novel
about a miserable kid who was sent to a summer camp
& at this camp
the boy had a counsellor who liked to torment & ridicule him
so the boy built a trap in the woods
& when the counsellor was lured
into the web of ropes & rendered powerless
the boy called him every degrading name
he'd ever wanted to
the counsellor just swore back
& threatened to beat hell out of him
when he got loose

the boy took a knife from his pocket
& gouged the counsellor's teeth out
stripped his pants
castrated him
waved cock & balls in the counsellor's face
then sewed them up in his mouth with fishing tackle
& the boy felt
truly happy
for the first time in his life

my mother & I were in the kitchen
the day after I took the aspirins
my stepfather was away on business

she told me not to tell anyone what really happened
"tell them it was food poisoning" she said
"spoiled pineapple juice" I said
& took a fresh can of it from the refrigerator
& poured it down the drain
a look of horror disappeared between us
we never mentioned it again

everyplace was a place
where no one knew
what they were doing
or why

keys to kingdoms

cold black night
sick & broke
big tough cliffie showed up
& knew where wine was free

down the street
another run-down rooming house
an old bootlegger sitting on his bed

"give this guy some wine!" cliffie said

the old man replied he didn't have any

"you better find some," said cliffie,
"or you're gonna wish you had some!"

"hey cliffie," I said, "it's all right, let's go!"

"you're not leaving until you get something to drink!"

then he grinned & told the bootlegger:
"this guy with me has a gun & he's gonna use it
if you don't find some wine!"

the old man moved from his bed to his beat-up dresser
removed a pint of cheap wine
& a revolver

he placed the gun beside him & passed the wine to cliffie
who handed me the bottle & commanded: "drink!"

I tilted the bottle & guzzled
closely watching the old bootlegger's hands

when the bottle was empty cliffie & I left

a couple of nights later I was lying in bed
drunk & broke

big tough cliffie came into my room with his friend jimmy
& said:
"let's go get some more wine!"

but this time jimmy pinned the old man's arms
cliffie pulled a knife & said:
"I'm going to have to carve you up
because you don't have any wine
& you don't have any money!"

he swept the knife
past the bootlegger's eyes
& feinted with it
laughing
when the old man flinched away
shaking & trembling

"please cliffie," he pleaded, "I'll get you some tomorrow!
please just let me alone!"

cliffie handed me the knife & said:
"this guy's gonna cut your throat!"

the knife blade
against his quivering skin
& the fear flooding from him
made me drunker
deeper than I'd ever been

we took turns with the knife
threatening & laughing at
the old white-haired man
before leaving him
uncut
his t-shirt soaking wet

3 days later
richard who lived in the room across from mine
& called himself "satan"
came into my room & said:
"go help cliffie, he's carrying some beer."

on the sidewalk I headed towards cliffie
& passed through several young white guys
standing in front of the old bootlegger's house
& one of them said:
"this is the guy who put a knife to my grandfather's balls!"

they surrounded me

I said: "I don't know what you're talking about!
I don't even know your grandfather!"

I looked at big tough cliffie
he gave me a big grin
& kept walking

a guy peeling off his jacket said: "I'm gonna fuck you up!"

I thought of hitting him while his arms were trapped
inside his jacket sleeves

instead I backed up against a parked car

laid on the hood
bent my legs
& covered up with my arms

their fists pounded me

but before any serious damage could be done
a police car roared around the corner
& onto the sidewalk beside us

I walked quickly into my rooming house
& sat down on the bed in richard's room

cliffie was laughing at me

2 cops stomped up the stairway
demanding i.d. from everyone

richard had warrants out
under his real name
so gave them fake i.d.

the police examined
hatchets & knives & pellet guns we used for target practice
on the walls & furniture

one of the cops said to me: "I want to see your room!"

& when he did he said: "oh my god!
this is the filthiest room I've ever seen!"

"there was a fire in here the other day," I said,
"a lot of water was thrown around,
& I haven't had a chance to clean it up."

richard'd smelled smoke
I'd passed out with a lit cigarette
& he saved my life
heaving pails of water
over me
the bed   the walls
everything

the cop poked carefully
through the stinking mess of ashes & wet clothes
he gave me a hard look & said:

"if that old man files charges
I'm coming back for you
& you're going away
for assault with a deadly weapon
& attempted murder!"

"I don't even know him!" I said

& stayed sober in bed the next 2 days
sick & weak & reflecting with shame
upon the torture of the old man
& cliffie's practical jokes

then richard's ex-wife spent the night with him

she once told me how much she hated richard
for treating her so cruelly when they were living together
"he owes me!" she said

& richard often told me how much he still loved her
& how wounded he was by her rejection of him

I walked down the hallway to use the bathroom in the
morning
& glanced inside richard's room
his ex-wife was stuffing a 5-dollar bill into her handbag

when richard returned that night
he yelled for me to come into his room
I yelled back that I was too sick to move

"you better get in here!" he shouted, "I want to talk to you!"

I got up
crossed the hallway
& sat down on his bed

"what's going on?" I asked him

alex was also in the room
& all alex ever wanted to do
as far as I could tell
was hurt somebody

"I left a 5-dollar bill on my dresser this morning," richard
said,
"now it's gone & I want to know who took it!"

"it wasn't me," I said, "I don't know who took it."

"I think you did," richard said,
"& I'm going to find out if you're lying or not!"

before I could make a move
he wrapped my long hair
around one of his fists
& placed the tip of a knife against my jugular vein

alex pressed the blade of a hunting knife
against my throat

"now tell me the truth!" richard demanded,
"I'll know if you're lying or not & if you are I'll kill you!"

he yanked hard on my hair & stared crazily into my eyes

"can I cut him?" alex asked eagerly

"wait until I know if he's lying or not!" richard answered

"I did not take your money," I said, "I am telling you the truth!"

"he's lying!" alex squealed, "I'm gonna cut him!"

"no," richard said, removing the knife,
"he's not lying. let him go."

I locked my door
& had barely crawled back into bed
when richard wanted me to return

"I'm sick!" I shouted, "I'm trying to sleep!
I'm not getting up again!"

"if you don't open your door!" he screamed,
"I'll know you took the money!"

I yelled: "please leave me alone!"

richard started chopping the door with his hatchet
splinters & chips of wood
began spitting into my room

I heard something at the window
looked up & saw alex
kneeling on the roof ledge
prying the latch with the hunting knife

it'd be moments before they invaded
& richard in his drunken fury wouldn't hesitate
to sink his hatchet into me
& alex'd happily stab me as many times as he could

a large coke bottle was lying empty on the floor
I thought to smash it through the window into alex's face
then grind it into richard when he came through the door

I reached for the bottle
but just as I grasped it
let it fall

& sank down on the bed
deciding I wouldn't move a muscle to save myself
but said silently:
"please let this violence stop!"
& my fear
became a calm night-blue mountain pool

I heard a shout
turned my head
& saw alex slip off the 2nd-storey ledge
& disappear

richard's hatchet stopped demolishing my door
the rooming house became quiet as it had ever been
I fell asleep easily

in the morning
tapping softly
richard woke me saying:
"I've got a cup of tea & a cigarette for you."

I got out of bed & opened the door

richard gave me the tea & cigarette

"I had to take alex to the hospital last night," he said,
"he cut his arm on the fence in the front yard
& had to get some stitches."

"well," I said, at least half-seriously,
"I'm glad he didn't get hurt any worse."

"he lost my hunting knife when he fell," richard said,
"I can't find it & it's your fault because you wouldn't open the door!"

& when he left to buy another knife

I walked away from that rooming house

feeling lucky

still unaware

of the keys

my heart

carried

for the kids who kill themselves because of braces

in elementary school the social studies teacher assigned seats according to test scores & the kids with the most correct answers were rewarded with seats closest to the teacher's desk

the competition was intense for those first few seats & always between the same white middle class kids who wore the only braces & owned the only cashmere sweaters

& though all of us learned we were given many opportunities to change our individual positions in the classroom there were no spectacular improvements nor unexpected failures

so I was prevented from sitting beside my best friend libby lutch because test results & guilt & fear kept me in the first dozen or so seats while libby sat somewhere in the deep end distant from the teacher's desk & attention

        with the other poor white
        & mexican kids
        whose seats were often
        empty
        while they were
        stooped over in the fields
        picking
        tomatoes
        for those of us
        nearest the teacher's desk

> who were discussing
> early slavery
> in the
> united states

30 years later marie tells me she was always in the low-grade sections of classrooms in every elementary school she attended & referred to kids who looked like me as "the kids with braces" envying the prominent symbols of parental love & understanding so deeply that she came to hate her strong even teeth

& I thought
the braces
were in my mouth
to keep me
quiet
about the other
disfiguring
teeth
eating me up
inside

refuge

in a shotgun club
on dee-troit avenue
plaster-cracked
spider-wino-man climbing the walls
jitterbug joint
except plugged-in in back
playing mostly to themselves
4 old black guys
blowing resurrection blues

the drummer
his kit fixed like a japanese landscape
& his 200 songs
was the first poet I ever knew

& the larger-than-life-sized
sweat-soaked
lead singer
would just smile at me & say

"don't worry white boy
we won't let nobody bother you
just come on back
& listen to the blues!"

drapetomania

you have to pack so fast you can't feel or
think about the pain you're fleeing strengthening
& yeah that's your thumb stopping a
beat-to-shit station wagon with diapers baby
shoes & a stuffed lion on the dashboard the
back seat splashed with clothes a janitor
running from ohio his wife & 5 kids & outside
chicago cold carbon wind blinding headlights
& a ride of a thousand miles with a mexican
trucker scabbing a load of steel & porno with
sawed-off shotgun & reinforced grille & hank
snow singing "who's gonna love you when your
ramblin days are done?" & windshield wipers
like giacometti sculptures wiping arkansas
fog west & you end up dead-broke in dallas on
sunday evening lost between industrial & re-
union streets attracting cops & creeps until
reaching a salvation army flop with a hundred
others & a kid on the next cot cries out loud
all night long

new home

instead of going to prison or killing vietnamese
an attic room in toronto on george street with
lead-paint-peeling-walls-falling-apart a bare
light bulb blazing & a disembodied voice speaking
each night at the foot of my bed so cynically it
might've been the world's own master of ceremonies
instead of the amplified speech of a burned out
emcee coming from the strip joint on dundas street
"ALL RIGHT!" the voice boomed "LET'S HAVE A BIG
HAND FOR THE LITTLE LADY!" & that's all I ever
heard besides rats in the walls & traffic moving
like a stacked deck being shuffled no angelus of
cash registers or applause just that emcee's voice
& moaning coming from the floor below from mary
a torrent of tangled black hair surging around her
waist framing her sunken blue-boned face like
furious tides around a violated moon where her
eyes fled like frightened animals mary lurching
through piss & shit & flies the floors & walls
hallucinating mary shaking with disease &
dissipation & moaning like the soul of nature dying
"LET'S HAVE A BIG HAND FOR THE LITTLE LADY!"

       exiled
       in a city
       of the future

dreams in the americas

I woke up sweating dreaming
about children carrying guns & hungry bellies
through brilliant green & crimson
salvadorean jungles
& I woke up thinking
about 2 young fugitives
I drove around the city last night
& the girl showed me scars
from the times she'd been raped
& the bones her father broke
& said "pain doesn't bother me anymore"
& laughed
describing teachers beaten over the head with her chair
& cops she'd bitten
& kids cold-cocked in the shopping malls
& how she kicked the bulldaggers in jail

I stopped the car outside an apartment
where the courts put her baby
after taking it away from her
she was inside a few minutes
& returned in tears
about the place smelling & looking like shit
"they don't take care of my baby!" she said
& remembered she was supposed to be in court yesterday
for assault charges
or some others
but "mostly" she said "they want to know where he is"—

her boyfriend sitting next to her
who'd stolen a supervisor's key
unlocked a window
& hitchhiked 300 miles
sleeping under bridges & in freezing open fields
to get here to her

& already has a job in a restaurant
fake i.d.
& shoot-to-kill coming when they catch him—
a body builder
armed robber
& dope dealer
barely alive when the law first got hold of him—
a child dying from
malnutrition
dehydration
& anemia

"it's the little kids younger than us"
the boy said
"who are really scary"

guilty as charged

in the morning the coral snake colours of the scapegoat hookers & the hyper street-talk of the other misdemeanors joy-lifted the courtroom atmosphere considerably.

I was up for disorderly conduct & possession of an illegal weed.

the judge, a pale faced crystal ball in black robes, said to me, "and what do you do with your life?"

"write poems," I said.

"write poems!" he yelped, as though I'd pissed on his foot.

"and how do you support yourself while you write these po-ems?"

"well," I said, "there's a woman who..."

"ohhh," he said. "I see."

"since you write po-ems," the judge went on, "why don't you recite one for us?"

& with that the courtroom quieted all the way down, like a noose with ears around my neck.

"I don't know," I stammered, "I don't think I can, I mean, I don't feel that I..."

"well!" snapped the judge, "I thought if you wrote po-ems, you'd at least be able to..."

"and so do I!" I said, surprising myself.

30 / LONESOME MONSTERS

"this is an early one," I told the court, "it's called 'pour mes amis,' and that's french, it means 'for my friends' ..."

"yes, yes," the judge said, "just get on with it."

"okay," I said & launched into the only one I could remember:

> "my dark heart weaves
> its dancing grief through you
>
> "and dreams into agony
> a rage fumbling above
> the blood-blackening of the abyss
>
> "rage enough to shunt the spell
> of insubstantial days and nights
>
> "rage remaking each limitation
> for an endless gathering
> stolen from tears
> whose tapestry bridges equators
> with rage of creation!"

the judge looked at me & said, "I suppose by that you mean the whole world's against you?"

"oh no," I said, "it just means there's a rage in the heart of human change ..." & I was going to say a lot more, but the judge said, "sentence suspended, I waive the court costs, you're free to go."

outside the courtroom a hooker was saying, "I never heard nothin like that before."

neither had I, a poem worth $250 & several months.

4 weeks later, I had the same judge & the same charges. this time he didn't ask me what I did, let alone how I managed to do it.

he gave me 6 months in jail & I wondered if he remembered me at all.

but when he said, "you're of no use to society," I was certain the judge knew who I was.

historical site

a phone booth on ossington avenue
where denise mackintosh
marie's friend
was strangled by her boyfriend
outside a crowded laundromat
of spectators

the same phone booth
I'd used to call marie
when she & I
first became
lovers

4 haiku

I pull the cord
night disappears
roaches run everywhere

■ ■ ■

NOT SAFE TO OCCUPY
posted on the doorway
of my home

■ ■ ■

lois in the big smoke
homeless and broke
in a wheelchair

■ ■ ■

I broke in here to sleep
but can't sleep
   ...listening...

love poem

remember that night all night when I sat on my hands &
    sweated & watched the clock's hands not move
    towards 5:30 or those nights you sat in
    shadows worn out but vigilant for fear of me
    passing out & setting the house on fire killing
    you & me & your kids & the cat or falling out of
    a window staggering to the bathroom like I did
    that time or just snapping all moorings and
    going berserk?

remember when 5:30 finally arrived & down to the hillbilly
    bar for shots & beers just to get me well & you
    smiled & bud powell incredibly came on the
    television & I forgot I'd ever been sick & was
    doing just what I wanted to be doing more than
    anything else & then left at 8 & got lost &
    panicked in the middle of the sidewalk with
    traffic blasting me & little kids going to school
    surrounding me & staring & your hand out of
    nowhere soft on my shoulder brought me back?

remember how I drank & passed out & drank & passed out
    all that day & decided at 3 in the morning to go
    to new orleans with a pocket full of librium &
    nothing else & then tore up the admitting room
    at the nuthouse at 5 & they strapped me down
    & I went into deetees & accused you of all
    manner of ill deeds & betrayal?

remember when I was released on an afternoon pass &
    with the sky the trees the sun exploding we
    made the most beautiful love while a cool gentle
    breeze dried our bodies that glorious sober day
    & when the inmates on the ward asked me what
    we did I started to tell them but they just
    groaned & walked away?

remember my dear those days & nights
    other days & nights
    made seem like
    the least
    of what we had?

hank

hank told me she was going to kick the shit out of me
        if I didn't stop drinking
she was wearing her dark sunglasses
        & a t-shirt reading KILLER DYKE
hank's a big woman with strong arms & shoulders
        & once stabbed a man 14 times
then called an ambulance & the police
        & stopped the man's bleeding
she'd been a medic in the navy
        but hank would've died in her cell that night
hallucinating & shaking
        if it hadn't been for an old black woman
who fed her chocolates & held her close

in court hank's own lawyer told the judge
        hank was a danger to society
& she was sent to a prison for the criminally insane
        where inmates were overdosed by the staff for kicks
to watch them spasming on the floor
        but police raided that institution
& arrested attendants & doctors for violence & theft
        & hank was transferred to a women's penitentiary
addicted to thorazine & nearly blinded by it
        & given a job painting buildings
on a ladder 60 feet in the air

hank's mother concealed her pregnancy
        & intended to abandon the newborn baby
in a garbage dump near their home

    but relatives intervened & took hank for their own
hank's new mother & father were both alcoholics
    & he raped & beat hank for several years
until hank's mother began dying
    then he took off
& hank dropped out of school
    to nurse her mother through the long misery
of a death by cancer & cirrhosis of the liver

hank's first arrest was for drunken bicycle riding
    at 9 years old
she'd gotten drunk after her only childhood friend
    had drowned while fishing with his father
the man hank stabbed in revenge
    many years later
when hank was wandering homeless in the winter
    in a sweatshirt & jeans
sleeping in the snow
    pissing her pants
drinking wine & hearing voices tell her what to do

hank'd been kicked out of the navy for being a lesbian
    kicked out with her lover
who said she'd always be there
    for hank
no matter what
    but slammed the door in hank's face
as soon as they were civilians

hank's only other friend had been her cellmate in the joint
    a woman who'd poured boiling grease
down her husband's throat

   for running around & beating on her
but hank found her hanging by the neck
   from their cell bars one afternoon

when hank finally made parole
   after 7 years
she refused it
   she couldn't imagine going from someplace bad
to somewhere better
   & was too hooked on their drugs to leave
but a year later hank left prison
   having withdrawn herself from the drugs
& worked painting houses & saved enough money
   to send herself to school
& obtain a degree in social work
   a job helping women in a battered women's shelter
& volunteer work helping drunks & addicts
   get free from their hells

when I last saw hank
   she was standing in a river at twilight
up to her waist in violet waves
   with a long fishing line cast out
(I thought)
   to catch other lost souls
& bring them to shore
   to help other lost souls
make it onto the shore

lonesome monsters

tommy 15 years old & dumped cold in july at a greyhound station by his father who handed him 60 dollars & said "make it on your own kid!" & so far tommy's made it to a government residence jammed with junkies & winos & hookers & thieves killing time & tommy's fat & retarded & always asking questions "where ya goin? what ya doin? can I go? what's the weather tomorrow?" we tell him "snow!" & tommy says "I don't have a coat! are you guys sure it's gonna snow?" & the guy we dragged drunk from the path of a semi-truck said "tommy if you had a fuckin brain in your head you'd know it doesn't snow in the summer for fuck's sake!" but the staff's called a meeting to straighten us out & the heavy metal kid shoves tommy & says to the supervisor "I wanna throw a flashbomb in your face!" & a kid whose mother murdered his father tells the new social worker "I want to suck your cunt!" & a young dopefiend says "don't ever call me a fag again!" to a tattooed teenage prostitute who asks the boy for a light & he holds the burning match against her breast & laughs when she screams & says to him "if only you didn't love me so much you wouldn't bother me!" & the ex-con ex-hockey player is showing off stabbing his nerve-dead leg with a lit cigarette & an old rummy tells tommy his father "oughta be shot with a ball of his own shit!" but compassion is scarce like the table scraps fed to the household pet

> swimming alone
> in the dining room fishbowl
> a piranha

reparation

I used to drive my mother
to a veteran's administration clinic
in ohio
& one day a guy was sitting in the waiting area
watching a pop machine repairman working
& the guy said

"that machine ripped me off
for 40 cents
I'm tired of gettin ripped off

"I was in world war 2
got shot in the ankle
got malaria
& a nervous breakdown
lost 48 men
& I'm tired of getting ripped off

"my son was sent to vietnam
& he's got agent orange
& a baby that's retarded
& I'm tired of gettin ripped off
I'm tired of it!"

& the repairman

gave him back

his 40 cents

after the strike

"cocksuckers work us like slaves!"
one lucky worker named tony says
& fakes an uppercut to the foreman's balls
swings a steel hook past his skull
stabs his finger with a lit cigarette
& the foreman retaliates
throwing cases of canned pop at all of us
over crates of milk coming down the track fast
backing us into the trailer

later tony says to me
"we got 6 men on 2 tracks
to do what 15 men on 3 tracks did before
the union sold us out
& the bosses hired a scab foreman & supervisor
fuckin stupid asses don't do nothin
I'd shove a milk jug down the foreman's throat
but I got a wife & kids!"

we hook drag shove & heave
thousands of cases of milk
in a huge freezing storage room
on a shift from midnight to dawn

I got there from a transient flop
when a man showed up from a day labour joint
& asked me if I wanted to make some money
"those places are thieves!" tony tells me
"they're robbin you!
those assholes sittin in some office

with a telephone doin nothin
makin more money off this job than you do!
somebody oughta stop that shit!"

so I work it
breathing sour milk
& when the break comes
I reach for a carton of orange juice
but tony tells me
"hell no!
you'll get us fired!
we can't have any!"
& points to the office

where we watch bosses
drink chilled juices

drifting

> "I have no ambition—unless negatively—
> I live continually in a reverie." —poe

> "I am what I am
> & what I was born to be
> hard luck is in my family
> & it's rollin down on me" —peetie wheatstraw

after the morning meal at the mission
  I drift through the city
    casing bookstores & stealing poems
      riding park benches & reading poe

drifting to a library listening room
  & peetie wheatstraw's "road tramp blues"

drifting I study the reality collages
  of sidewalk panels—
    smears of violent blood & panicked shit
      disgusted vomit & defiant piss
        newspaper pages of propaganda
          fragments of heart-breaking personal letters
            advertising fliers full of lies
              spontaneous arrangements of broken glass
                playing cards scattered like occult messages
                  feathers clothing cigarette butts & candy wrappers
                    the blue & orange chalk marks of city workers
                      names & curses & vows etched into the cement

drifting past pathetic parking lots
  & bleak residential streets

      I find a full-blown riot
        in front of a vacant house
          wild flowers & rebellious weeds
            exploding in purple & red & yellow & green
              small trees waterfalling leaves
                grasshoppers birds ants spiders
                  butterflies & bees
                    soaring buzzing crawling climbing
                      leaping & singing

drifting to make the last feed at a crosstown mission
  where a frail elderly woman
    wearing a white lace dress & blue bonnet
      splits fiercely territorial places in line
        as easily as spoons split the mission stew

drifting to a derelicts' park
  I lie down in the grass
    & watch clouds metamorphosizing overhead
      startled to hear the sharp sound of a fastball
        slapping the leather pocket of a baseball glove

an old man's winding up & cutting loose
  throwing to a young rummy who's staggering
    in & out of a catcher's crouch
      & returns the ball wildly over the old man's head
        the ball rolls through mud puddles & stops near me
          the old man on his way to retrieve it

wearing baggy grey pants
  an old sweatshirt & tennis shoes
    a faded baseball cap

     & carrying a shopping bag containing
      a fielder's glove
       & well-worn catcher's mitt
        & slices of bread from the sally ann
         & half-a-dozen baseballs
          some of them grass-stained black
           with covers torn & stitches dangling
            but it's his brand new 5-dollar ball
            that rolled through the mud

I wipe the ball off & hand it to him
  & ask him if he needs another catcher
  but he says he's through for the day

"it's a long season" the old man says
  "I pitch in parks all over the city
   I been learnin to pitch for 7 years now
    decided to pick it up when I turned 60"

"you sure have a smooth delivery" I tell him
  & he grins out of his white-whiskered sun-wrinkled face
   & mentions books on pitching he's studied
   & pitchers he's managed to study in person

"my friends tell me I'm crazy" he says
  "they say nobody's a baseball pitcher at my age
  they say I'll never make it
   but I don't want to make it
    I just want to pitch
     & my arm's getting stronger every year
      & my fastball's getting faster!"

I drift back across the city

    to another park
      in time for the twilight hour
        of silence & bums & lovers
          & remember lovers I've held & kissed
            on benches in this park for 20 years

the light blue sky turns dark night-blue
a breeze shakes the trees' shadows
  I breathe deeply & stretch my legs
    & say softly across the park
      "take a break pop"

to an old man in a ragged harness
  who's carefully pulling a shopping cart
    loaded with grocery bags & battered suitcases
      sheets of wood & piles of rags
        & coats & sweaters & stacks of newspapers

he stops a moment
  & takes a long look at something far away
    then picks up his harness again
      as artificial lights flash on
        & machines chase each other around the park

I drift through crowded avenues
  where people are looking for something consuming
    where 2 young white boys are chasing a black kid
      back & forth across a traffic jammed street

the black kid's running easily
  sticking his arm out & spinning around light poles
    going abruptly in the opposite direction
      not really trying to get away

the bare-chested white boys are in furious pursuit
  especially the boy with blood streaming down his face
    he's so angry he's out of control
      slipping & sliding & falling down
        in front of taxi cabs screeching their brakes
          in front of tourists gasping & gaping

the black kid runs right into the doorway of a pizza joint
  trapping himself
    & the white boys throw punches & swing their boots
      the black kid looks done for

but springs free of them all
  & dances down the sidewalk
    shaking his finger
      & laughing
        at the white boys after him again
          but the black kid vanishes into the traffic—
            a young street-houdini

a friend of mine drifts by
  & tells me he bought a new knife
    & was just standing in a doorway
      trying to read the knife's inscription
        when a policeman arrested him for assault

"the cop testified he was 10 feet away" said my friend
  "& I didn't move my feet
    so how could I be lunging at him?"

I toll him I have no idea
  how intentions so innocent
    could be so badly misconstrued

he invites me to share his room for the night
  full of roaming cockroach herds
    & crazed drunks next door
      & an empty closet from which
        his few belongings were stolen

"you can sleep on the floor" he offers
  but I say "no thanks"
    then we shake hands & grin
      thinking of the line at the mission
        in the morning

I drift towards my bed
  a private suite
    a hillside jungle of trees & bushes
      in one of the wealthiest neighbourhoods in the world
        so exclusive the residents don't have to
          carry their garbage to the street

it just gets up
  & walks away on its own
    I laugh to myself

& drift toward dreams
  a white crescent moon
    drifting across
      my blanket of smiling angels' eyes
        & beautiful azure sky

one year to the next

ricky hood from next door's pounding on our door he's on parole & wine & valium & playing an unplugged electric guitar & singing "UFOs over houston!" the rats are clawing wailing & hurling themselves against flimsy barricades I built to protect a last loaf of stale bread & fire engines scream through the black & yellow window the radio's reporting annual family holiday massacres & bottle-bombs thrown from the high-rise pressure cooker across sherbourne street explode on the sidewalk & smash sunroofs out of parked cars & young wingnuts are down the block wrecking storefronts fighting police a raggedy bum bellows "why light up city hall? blow it up!" & new year's day talks in its sleep complaining to no avail the ultraviolet blues of unbeaten emergencies in our home in hell in room 41 of a downtown misfits' hotel under renovation-siege new owners like toxic fires starting in the basement panicking every living thing painting the walls white & pink & I'm turning over a dead leaf with a glass of gut-burning tap water a handful of codeine & last night's butts for breakfast the top floor phantom's singing down the stairwell "losers make their own way!" a month ago marie & I were digging through garbage cans in brandon manitoba now we struggle through a long line for food we can't use without machinery we don't have & in front of us a friendly filthy young man wearing a thick bandage over a bad burn "passed out" he said "against a radiator" &

shoved up his shirt to reveal old wounds burned black &
purple to the bone & laughed & said "I'm into pain!"

        foodbank-footsteps in the snow
        melting through roses
        fading on the carpet

social services

little boy in a stroller blows a yellow horn
skinny street dog trots past
old man counts his pension money
3 rough & hungry men give it the eye
a guy sweeps the sidewalk with a ragged broom
I'm waiting on a welfare worker
grey hot & toxic sky
streetcar crashes by
kids sing "fuck the schools!"
a truck full of bananas
rasta bums a match
big black hearse
shiniest thing on the street
one-legged old man with a white beard
drags his crutches
cops go into a jewelry store
where's that welfare worker?
little red-headed boy with a plastic gun
asks me about the punk band
that practices in the basement
I'm rolling cigarettes
& when she shows up
she tells me she was stabbed by delinquent girls
on her last job
so I
try to be of as much help to her as I can

reality for rent

cheap & clean
in the old woman's house
hunched between larger houses
like she is between people
at 81
gnome-like
an arthritic hump wrenching her back

she lives with her ex-husband
a parkinson's victim she let move back in
when he got sick
& she has to rent a room
to almost
make
it

she has latches chains bolts & bars across the
doors & says

               "I'm so afraid
               always
               every day
               I'm so afraid!"

afraid if I turn on a light I'll burn the house down
afraid if it snows the roof will cave in
afraid if I use the phone I'll call hong kong direct

she's so afraid she can't sleep

afraid my kidneys are bad & I'll wear out the carpet
going back & forth to the bathroom
afraid if I wash my face
the water bill will soar

she's afraid of all this & more & tells me about it
barging into the room where I'm typing
yelling

                "I can't stand it!"
                "what?"
                "that barking machine you got there!"

then she tells me to check the traffic
& see if any of the cars speeding out of control
are about to crash
into the front of her house

getting culture

they troop us from a group house to a play
little ducklings 2 by 2
the social workers fresh from college
heading a delinquent & derelict processional
for a torpid play about the untorrid life
of a provincially strait-jacketed woman
translated from the french & written by a man
a play coming at us from a great distance

I sit down front row centre knees rubbing the stage
beside doug the skinny grizzled old bootlegger
who's got the lack-of-wine bad shakes
it's his very first play

& in a very early scene
the girl's brother snatches her doll
stabs it
& she all-of-a-sudden
screams
right-at-us
jolting doug sky high off his seat
into an emphysemic cement-mixer coughing fit
& he gasps out loud:
"no wonder my nerves are bad!"

the play's as long as life is short
& every bit as absurd
with no intermission
& many kidneys at high tide
a million nicotined cells calling for help

so doug clambers up in clumsy cowboy boots
stumbling hacking wheezing clattering
through the small theatre's full house
eclipsing the spotlight
& announces by way of explanation:
"I have never been so bored in my life!"

finally it ends
she dies
& outside I ask doug what he thinks
of his very first play

"they'll never get me to another one"
he says
"I feel like I been dragged through an asshole
& fed farts for a week!"

it was the finest theatrical criticism
I've ever heard

propaganda

gathering before dawn
on a skid row sidewalk
waiting for vans to arrive
with drivers who'd hire us
to deliver advertising newspapers
door to door
in far distant suburbs
for a very few dollars

it was daylight
when we were dropped off in pairs
into instant communities
where the early morning dew & mud pools
soaked our feet
& the bag we carried the papers in
became heavier & heavier
while we walked
with legs aching
& tongues drying out
to stick extravagant lies
into someone's front door

we covered endless neighbourhoods
where successful people
came & went or worked on their lawns

at the end of the ordeal
my partner & I sat down on a curb
waiting for the van to pick us up
& he told me

about his wife & 3 children
cramped into
a couple of rundown & expensive rooms

he'd been an officer
in the iranian air force
10 years for the shah
& 7 with khomeini
but had finally wearied
of all of the trouble
& knew
in north america
there was plenty to eat
nice places to live
& exceptional personal freedom
but he'd had to haul advertising
every day
to barely feed his family

he was a small quiet & serious man
with eyes sad & distressed
but mostly confused
because of the advanced technical skills he possessed
nobody would employ

"I thought it was supposed to be better here"
he kept saying
softly
& shaking his head

"in iran" he said
"if we were doing this job

the people would invite us into their homes
& give us plenty of water to drink
& something to eat
but here
they don't even see you"

3 haiku

my poems in a library
tonight
I sleep in the wind

■ ■ ■

police
come with sledgehammers
the door is open

■ ■ ■

in line in the rain
at the food bank
a child screams

houses of the dying

in a north american suburb
a major social event is going on—

plastic collection buckets are being passed
around a masonic auditorium
to a mostly well-fed & fashionably dressed audience

a successful man is on stage
asking for more & more money
but his pitch is cut short
by the unexpected entrance of the woman we've all come to see
a little old woman wearing sky-blue
who says:

"if I'd known there was going to be a collection taken
I'd never have agreed to be here
I don't want your money
I want you to give something that hurts
I want you to give love
in your own homes"

her voice unlike any I've ever heard
calming me deep down
where I'm seldom calm

she tells a story
about a long-haired kid in england
whose father demanded the boy get a haircut
& told his son that if
he didn't go directly to a barber shop

he'd cut the boy's hair himself
the boy pleaded & begged & tried to explain
his father was unyielding
the boy left the house
& was found the next day
on railroad tracks
decapitated

"I want you to see the suffering christ in everyone"
she says
"in the delinquent child
in the alcoholic sick in the streets of the world
in the drug addict
prostitute
welfare mother
& next door neighbour"

& I thought of homes I've known:
houses of the dying whose motto is to see & feel no pain
the home my father abandoned only to be jailed where he hanged himself
the home my mother fled to make manic & suicidal escape attempts
the home where my aunt shot my grandmother
& turned the gun on herself
the homes of my closest high school friends:
where tom's mother overdosed in her 40s after years of breakdowns
where jim's mother drank herself to death in her early 50s
where chuck's mother began crying & couldn't stop
or set the table for invisible guests

so she'd have someone to talk to
but she'd ended up locked up in another psych ward
& the home of my friend lance smith
where he shot himself in the head with his father's shotgun

& I thought of homes I've abused
children I've abandoned
love I refused to give or be given
homes of broken humans I've hurt
while accusing them of harming me
& cold families I've known frozen into images of homes
& homes of open torture like storms from hell exploding
like the home marie came from
where she was beaten kicked raped & strangled

"I want you to give something that hurts"
said the little old woman wearing sky-blue
"I want you to give love
in your own homes
I want you to see the suffering christ
in everyone"

probably

    get up early to drive to the veteran's administration hospital in ann arbor & first thing I'm facing laverne & shirley loud filmed live & pat my mother says "I finished that book on francis farmer last night" I say "you did?" pat says "yeah am I glad it isn't so easy to get somebody locked up now when I go crazy or I'd never get out" we both laugh both shaking chain-smoking hunched over like inmates on a ward "poor francis farmer" pat says "those soldiers coming over from that army base to the hospital & raping her every weekend" "yeah" I say "yeah" pat raped by a drunken bar pick-up in front of me when I was 4 & a cop rammed a long slender metal flashlight up my ass outside los angeles "didn't know whether to jump you or rape you" he said

    so we're in the car a hot morning in december foggy raining mist a full moon dawn lights highway 23 past the federal correctional institution "they're expanding that joint" I tell pat she says "oh yeah?" on past the maximum security mental health facility 'prison area don't pick up hitchhikers' past the state maximum security prison for women amid flat desolate fields spray-painted graffiti on an overpass bridge 'devil children pbb acid rain they love it' trucks passing drowning the subaru pat nervous kicking the plastic pitcher of piss she's bringing for tests & says "I guess I'm scared of trucks from the time we ran into one when I was a little girl in illinois" I say "yeah there's a lot to be scared of from those guys" truckers telling me they like to shake up people in small cars just for kicks pat growing up in 'little egypt' southern illinois her father in massacre of scab coal miners ku klux klan shooting it out with gangsters almost shooting my mother in her baby carriage the first aerial bombing in north america bootleggers dropping dynamite on the competition from a slow low-flying airplane black lung killing my grandfather who returned from going to vote one day & said "any time I have to walk over dead bodies to vote I'm gonna give it up" other relatives dying in cave-ins or stabbed to death or going to prison for theft

& pat's afraid there's more bad cheque warrants out for her & says "I'm not going back to jail no matter what" & I say "me neither" & pat says "but you probably will" & I say "yeah probably will" & both sigh then talk about when the f.b.i. showed up threatening pat with jail if she wouldn't tell them where I was & my sister leslie remembering special agents banging on the door & how cold they were & how stereotypical & just how nasty

outside this hotel a man is freezing to death

for preston blount

thrashing around seizing sleep dreaming frustration
waking with stomach clenching anxious fists switch
on the light cockroaches stampede a yellow skull
grinning in the black windowpane sweat-soaked sheets
wrapped like a strait-jacket alarm clock sawing time
into pieces wind howling shaking windows scarring
dust with its claws ceiling bleeding blood-red neon
from old hotel sign swinging outside sour-smelling
shit & wine piercing the air a relic from a previous
tenant an abandoned centrefold stained with dead
sperm feeding roaches I get up to use the
hallway toilet but somebody's strangled the week's
roll of paper overnight & left it in larva-like
clots over the piss-puddled floor cockroaches
cover the mirror suddenly a phantom a man
materializes behind me wearing a pair of socks & a
mustache a face full of wounds & floating eyes his
balls are larger than his biceps stalactite-hair
conceals the bones of his hopes his penis hangs like
a broken thumb & we terrify each other with how
alive we both are & in my room the milk has frozen
on the ledge the orange juice has blown into the
street & exploded

promenade park past midnight

the river
dull green murk
& drops of poison rain
from clouds like phantom footsteps
in a sky like fresh cement
no starlight or moonlight
red lights blink from skyscrapers like banks of computers
bare twisted trees
trucks over bridges like electrons through a tube
steam & smoke
a catfish splashes
windows like tombstones
a rat runs out of the shadows
& we both freeze
startled to find each other here
shivering in a gas-filled breeze
with the huge luminous owens-illinois sign
atop the highest building
a capital "I"
in the middle of a large zero
here
serenading

demolition derby

     in a pub on gibson's landing a guy was telling me his troubles about his packed suitcases stacked for a year at the front door & his bed on the couch & his wife's hostility & his children's dread-filled obedience

     when suddenly

his face was glowing & he was grinning

     he told me
     how he was going to do it
     drunk some night
     pedal to the floor
     lights out
     windows wide open
     bombs away
     but he said he wasn't going alone

he was going to smash his death
through the headlights
of someone else's life
at the exact moment
he chose

     "if I go out that way" I said to him
"I don't want to take anybody else with me."

     "you underestimate yourself"
     he said

a found poem of lucy b.

"I told my daughter
we are going to die together
life isn't worth living

"I covered the bed with gasoline
& set it on fire
the fire started
but I got up

"I heard my little girl cry
I tried to save her
but it was too late
I couldn't get near her
the flames were too high

"I loved my daughter
I was fed up with life
I had just moved
the refrigerator didn't work anymore
I had no money
& nobody wanted to help me"

down here

sunshine
on downtown eastside sidewalks
glows fresh crimson
like rose petals fallen
from ransacked gardens of the broken-hearted

from those who wear the violent evenings
        on faces bruised black & purple
        whose teeth are kicked through panicked mouths
        begging mercy
        whose sight is slashed blind by knives of
        darkness
        inside murdered souls
        whose lives are worn out demolitions
        in screaming alleys
        of vomit & unending misfortunes

& for those crawling drunk & sick
        into jaws of rabid doorways & handcuffs of the
        police

& for those who fall or get pushed or raving leap
        from caged-in hotel windows
        of desperation & hate & grief

& for those lining up more patient than saints
        in cold rain & seagull shit
        to receive crusts of bread

& for those sniffing glue
        beside railroad tracks of uselessness
        to derail a birthplace renovated into exile

& for those plunging needles
        through veins seeking ecstasy
        but flowing with nervous shame & misery

& for those whose scared runaway skin
        is sold without hope
        to hypocrisy's ghosts

& for those cheated by political schemes
        & are drowned in tidal waves of unknown
        committees

& for those hardened like steel
        by the arson of their childhoods'
        gentle visionary love of the real

& for refugees pouring in from the earth's economic wars

& for refugees fleeing wars in the roots of their hair

& for those strait-jacketed into numbers & things
        whose withered spirits don't interest
        the scientific god who has forsaken them

& for those smelling & looking like death
        staggering through whirling neon vertigoes
        of east hastings
        & whose leering faces are smeared with
        rejection

& for those run over by monstrous rush hours
        of mountains & skyscrapers of enormous wealth
        & who get busted for jaywalking
        a puddle of small debt

& for those whose lungs are wrecked
> in a quicksand
> of malnourished infested tubercular rent

& for those eaten by fears sending them reeling
> from a breeze turning a corner
> or a shadow thrown over them
> reminding them of all they've tried to forget

& for those whose inarticulate cries for help
> are thrown out like garbage
> arrived from hell

& for those who survive on what's tossed aside
> into gutters of abundance denied

& for those who have nowhere to be
> & no way to live
> & are somewhere naked & shaking
> with a life no one else could endure

& for those who are loneliness frozen in tiny rooms
> & whose mental rainbows of aliveness & joy
> are sucked dry by fragmenting screens
> of colour teevees

& for those overdosed on jealousy & bitterness
> for what might've been
> for the bad luck decades that've bitten them
> & whose frustrations carve wounds
> inside & out

& for those whose unshed tears are choking them
> or who can't stop crying
> & die of exposure

& for those who are nothing without a job
      & have no one to employ them except more trouble
      pushing them out on a limb
      & over the edge
      crushing the life out of anyone
      beneath them when they fall

& for those fighting terrorizing voices in their heads
      reviling betraying & possessing them

& for those who can't help driving everyone else
      away from them

& for petty sneak thieves stealing pieces of themselves

& for killers of plum trees & the moon

& for the abandoned & damned adolescents
      unleashing vandalism & fists of vengeance

& for those whose children are stolen
      by social cops
      & are driven mad by the anguish
      of unnatural loss

& for those peddling every remnant of innocence
      & pawning every friend belonging to them
      for another fix or a bottle
      creating a purpose
      out of a daily nothingness

& for those who've grown old
      & left behind a breath at a time
      but whose battered dignity
      is a victory of their own

& for those whose religion
>> is a lottery-bingo-longshot addiction
>> reversing their history & bringing salvation
>> but whose numbers never get picked or called
>> & whose horses never come through

& for those struggling to make
>> against all odds
>> an authentic personal change

& for those who can't stand to be alone
>> & can't stand to be known by anyone

& for those picking fights
>> out of a disabled desire
>> for human communion
>> & end up with their lives
>> & others' in ruins

& for those boasting of being on top
>> of what is obviously pinning them
>> to illusions of mutilated lightning

& for those dreaming plan after plan for escape
>> but haven't the means
>> to get through yesterday

& for those whose grip on a can of lysol
>> is at least a perilous future
>> of savage relief

& for those called parasites or pariahs or bums
>> but who give their last shirt
>> or pass a kind word

& for those whose love is crippled & twisted
   yet bursting to give
   but can find no one able
   to heal & receive it

& for those picking butts & fighting withdrawal
   with emergencies to get through
   on nothing but stoplights & starlight
   & 'to hell with it all!'

& for those who sentence themselves to die
   obsessed with bridges & razor blades
   & calculations of barbiturates & alcohol

& for those wandering day & night
   searching curbs & glances
   for wallets & miracles

& for those fed up & disgusted enough
   to live quietly
   out of shopping carts
   beneath viaducts
   or hidden in trees in the parks

& for those who've never known a moment's peace
   & are so dirty & ugly & mean
   it's worth time in the bucket
   to shatter self-satisfied expressions
   of tourists strolling by
   looking clean

& for those gripped by wheelchairs
   wobbling on canes
   lurching between crutches

of unremitting pain
& whose courage mocks a world
speeding by in disdain

& for those deliberately sabotaging
every attempt at helping themselves
adjust to a mass social madness
accurately perceived
as more insane than themselves

& for those trying to get by
& take care of a family
on little more than defiance & love
in overwhelmed & worried eyes

& for those collapsing in shadows
pissing their lives down the front of their pants

& for those whose tattoos & time dots
are the only possessions
that haven't been lost
or stolen from them

& for those talking only to birds & stones
& sweeping evil spirits from the air
with magical movements of their hands

& for those longtime lovers & partners
holding together
amidst years raining down upon them
a bad human weather

& for those the most frightening
fearing no one & nothing
after having fear kicked out of them

as soon as they could feel anything

for these
  my own
    my selves
      my tortured prey
        & degraded predators
          my sisters & brothers

let my words
  sing a prayer
    not a curse
      to the tragic
        & sacred mystery

of our
  beautiful
    suffering
      eternal worth

zoned residential

here
the people disappear themselves

snow on the ground rain coming down in the dead zone of night when cats scream like scalded babies & the lights are long turned off into paranoid dreams of real estate & bathroom renovation on a dark residential street an ambulance with siren blaring & red & white lights flashing stops outside & a stretcher covered by an orange blanket is taken into the house where an old couple live alone & the people nearest them in the whole world & reality of actual physical presence never wake up not that we're supposed to it's just how life is on this street forget it one of the old people is placed in the back of the ambulance beneath the orange blanket but I don't know if it's the old man or the old woman a dangerous situation mostly middle-aged middle-class couples with a kid or 2 a gynecologist geologist executive-photographer university professor bank teller factory worker massage therapist probation officer social worker one welfare bum & one neo-nazi convicted of distributing hate literature the kind of street where no one gives a damn if you live or die where no one would get out of bed to save your life unless your dying disturbed their sleep it looks boring & is but rambos with automatic rifles sometimes run the street hoping to make a human connection of some kind through the malevolent electro-magnetic fields dividing & isolating everyone so neatly into rigid individual territories of self-centred fear & greed while adjustment techniques make welfare bum or

bank employee equally useless as neighbours zoned
residential wearing tight grins & whistling in the daytime

      snow shovels scraping sidewalks
      graves being dug
      for everyone to come home to

no wonder I can't solve my problems

avoid alcohol
  spicy foods
  prolonged standing
  & overtiredness

keep
  dry & clean

adjust
  your habits

try to be regular

don't strain

insert nozzle
  all the way
  into
  your
  rectum

do this
  each morning & evening

they tell me

& that's just to deal with

hemorrhoids

Killing Yourself and Living Through It

Gunshots outside in the darkness! Louder! Closer! The downstairs door explodes! Thunder on the stairway! Screams! Then they're in the bedroom. Rifles aimed right at me. I smile, make a quick move with my hand under the blanket, and they do it for me—some North American death squad, in Point Place, Ohio . . . .

Floorboards creaked and I saw Alice standing next to the bed. She slid her hand beneath the blanket and gently squeezed my penis. It jerked and shrivelled like it'd been bitten by an eel.

"Come on honey," she said, "it's almost New Year's. Get up soon and join the party, okay?"

"Alice," I said, "it's a hell of a thing to kill yourself and live through it."

She put her hand on her hip and stared at me. "Gee, hon," she said. "I don't know. I guess it is. But hurry up, okay?"

Darlene, her sister, yelled from the living room, "Hey, Crash! When we gonna get a look at you?" And they all laughed.

I reached for the glass of water on the table next to the bed and my ribs burst into flames.

There was a moment, just before I steered the car into the wall, when I felt ecstatic about ending my life. The next thing I knew, a surgeon was hovering above me picking glass out of my face. I thought, 'Osborn, you are in more trouble than the trouble that caused you to kill yourself in the first place.'

I reached in slow motion for one of the red capsules the surgeon told me contained the strongest pharmaceutical dosage of codeine. I slipped it into my mouth and washed it down with water. It occurred to me that if I'd had a supply of these pills beforehand, I'd never have smashed myself into a wall at 60 miles an hour. They would've been something to live for.

Finally, I eased myself out of bed and shuffled into the living room.

"The return of the mummy!" Darlene hooted at me.

My head was wrapped so thickly with bandaging it looked like I was wearing a swollen turban. My right leg, wrapped with tape around and around the knee area, resembled a pumpkin. Steel pins jutted out of broken fingers.

They were using Hall and Oates on television for music, so, in what proved to be my friendliest contribution to the festivities, I put a Dead Kennedys' record on the stereo and let it play, despite shrieks of protest, until I heard the line: "I'm looking forward to death!" screamed again and again . . . .

Besides Alice and her sister, both friends of mine since childhood, Darlene's boyfriend, Raymond the body builder, was there. Darlene bailed him out of jail for New Year's after having him locked up for assaulting her on Christmas. He looked at me solemnly and said he'd bring some protein powder for me the very next day. "It'll help you a lot," he said.

Darlene complained that all Raymond did was eat, go to the gym, eat, and go to the gym and work out. "He won't even talk about lookin' for a job!" she said. I liked Raymond.

"How many charges ya got?" he asked me.

"Three," I said, and he smiled approvingly.

"He got one of them in the Emergency Ward," Alice said,

"for calling the cops 'cocksuckers' and 'motherfuckers'. Laying there with blood all over him, yelling at the cops...." Darlene and Raymond laughed.

"They saved my life," I explained to Raymond, "against my will." He nodded as though he understood, then broke into a gap-toothed grin and shouted, "Well, shit, Happy New Year, ya old bastard!"

Then when Alice and Darlene were in the kitchen, I overheard Alice say, "I don't understand what Bud's so upset about."

I wondered what the matter was with these people that they didn't comprehend the gravity of my situation.

So I played cards begrudgingly, snorted a little cocaine, smoked some pot, and scowled, listening to Alice announce over and over that this was going to be THE year for each one of us. THE year when everything finally turned out all right.

Joey, another friend of ours, kept the phone ringing, calling to let us know whenever the song "Sexual Healing" was playing on the radio.

Joey was spending New Year's whacked on valium, raking his frozen front yard, and trying to decide whether or not he should find the bisexual cop who obsessed him, and who threatened to shoot Joey if he ever saw him again.

Darlene and Raymond left as the year's first day dawned grey as the edge of a razor blade.

Alice chopped up the last lines of coke. She was at the raw end of a long drunk and her nerves were blowtorched.

We inhaled the powder and sat down on the couch.

"Take one of these codeine pills," I told her, "it'll cool you right out."

She shook her head and began crying.

"What's the matter?" I asked her.

"Your shoes," she said, sobbing now.

"My shoes?"

"Remember when I was scrubbing the blood off your shoes when I brought you back here from the hospital?"

"Yeah, what about it?" I said. The astonishment I felt watching Alice's frenzied cleaning was the first feeling besides rage and terror I'd had since I discovered I was alive.

"I did it because they reminded me of that doctor's shoes," Alice said.

"What doctor?"

"When I had the operation."

"Oh, yeah."

"At the abortion clinic."

"What?"

"The doctor had blood on his shoes like yours did," Alice said.

"You had an abortion?" I said. "That was the operation you've been talking about?"

Alice nodded.

"What happened?"

"It was horrible," she said.

"It hurt?"

"It hurt a lot and it still hurts. When I went there, there were people carrying signs saying 'Baby Killer' and screaming at me."

"Jeezus," I said, "that's awful. Did you go by yourself?"

"No," Alice said, "Joey went with me, but I asked you to go with me because I thought you could understand and help me get through it."

Dark circles of fatigue and streaks of smeared eyeliner surrounded her light-blue eyes.

"Well," I said, "didn't Joey..."

"Joey!" Alice yelled. "You know Joey!"

"It's what I been trying to tell you about drinking," I said. "When you told me about the abortion and asked me to go with you I was in a blackout, and you just kept calling it 'the operation' after that and I didn't want to tell you I didn't know what you were talking about, but if I'd known it was an abortion you were talking about...."

Alice stopped crying and stared at me.

I stretched my right leg out and grimaced a little.

"What did I say when you told me about it?"

Alice gave me a deadly look. "You said the guy didn't hold a gun to my head, so what was I complaining about."

"I said that?"

Alice nodded.

"Hell, I'm sorry," I said, "but that's what I mean. Alcohol's a poison, and it poisons your brain so you say evil things and you don't remember any of it."

At that Alice's head fell forward as though she'd been axed in the neck. Tears poured down her face.

"Is that why we don't fuck," I asked her, "because it still hurts?"

"Yes," Alice said, very quietly.

"But," I said, "you bring home all these guys you hate from the bars and let them fuck the shit outta you?"

She nodded, and covered her face with her hands.

I got up, hobbled to the bathroom, shut the door, and pissed in the sink while looking at my reflection in the mirror.

'You sure are one lucky guy,' is what the doctors and nurses had told me.

street theatre

at the corner
  a woman sits on the curb
    wearing several sweaters & a couple of coats
      she's arranging shopping bags around her
        then gets up
          & goes into a telephone booth

she chats awhile
  then listens at length
    she lectures
      & winces at some insensitive reply
        she complains
          she trembles a moment with terror
        & suddenly
          pickpockets hope from the air
            & her black eyes
          shine

she casually traces the shelf
  with her fingers
    or works them together with anxiety & worry
      next they take flight
        frenzied flamingos
          & she unfolds like an enormous accordion
        playing rainbows of laughter
          until interrupted
            by some capsizing comment
          that reddens her eyes
            with grief so powerful

             her body shakes
               like a wave torn from the sea
             sobbing
                across deserts

then her face drops a curtain
  she heaves a big sigh
    leaving her transparent theatre
      & expressionlessly
        slumps to the curb & her backstage bags
          & stares across the street
            where neon revolves
          meaninglessly

she reaches into a paper sack
  removes a piece of bread
    & chews it slowly
      exhausted
        from giving the heart of her truth
          to the well of the phone
            where it fell without splashing
          endlessly

for she never
  dropped
    a
      dime

community life

a short block from the gigantic shopping mall
advertising itself as "the heart of the city"
is a little vest-pocket "community park"
with some wooden benches
a couple of trees
& a small fountain
with a large thunderbird sculpture in the middle

2 dirty long-haired indians
are sitting on a bench
a few feet from sidewalk & street
beneath 20 or 30 carbon-coloured leaves
hanging from an anorexic tree
& they're passing a bottle of cheap wine
& trying to conceal it at the same time
but a suit & tie white guy
who was just passing by
has taken the trouble to get 2 cops off yonge street
& direct them against the indians

one of the cops grabs the bottle
out of the older indian's raggedy coat
& the other cop jams his hands
into the other indian's pants pockets

the bottle is 3/4s full
when the cops pour it out
& tell the indians:
"it's against the law to drink in public"
then swagger back to yonge street

the indians check their pockets for change
the old one's limping around & swearing
the other one asks me if I saw what happened

"it was terrible" I said

"now I have to go back down that hole & bum some more!"
& the indian makes his hand into a fist
leans toward me & says:
"no wonder fuckin cops get hit!"

"you're right" I tell him
& watch them descend into the subway

I get up & walk across victoria street
past a crowd
of young well-groomed white university students
sitting at shaded tables on the sidewalk
drinking expensive beers & wines
with a tiny white grillework fence of privacy
keeping them safe
from the perils of a community park

3 haiku

black man in cold rain
opening a garbage can
christmas morning

■ ■ ■

"he broke my teevee set!"
"how?"
"when I banged his head on it!"

■ ■ ■

who do you
panhandle
for real change?

something's going around

ginger told me she can't do it anymore
like she could when she didn't care
but now she can't breathe

                the bathroom she's hiding in
                is smothering her
                the tiles like a demon's teeth
                grinning
                closing in
                on her heart   pounding

it used to be like nothing
she could let go & drift
dreaming of white sand beaches

                warm salt water
                licking her clean

or making lists of what she'd do tomorrow
the laundry
connecting with her dealer

                but right now
                even her cigarette is sweating
                & ginger regrets flushing the pills
                pouring out the booze
                wishes she had SOMETHING

she's paralyzed with fear
someone is carving her up inside
she's crying tears she's never cried before
so hysterical she's laughing

        it's too much all of a sudden
        ginger's wringing wet
        she's burning up

but has to go out there
it's all she's known
since a rag merchant set her up
so many years ago

        but with speed it was always so easy
        & the glue kick
        wearing cowboy boots & a silk nightgown
        glue dried on her face in black patches
        telling a cabbie 'take me to the glue store!'

never before has ginger felt
how much she hates them
but what else can she do?
a waitress worn out with varicose & dime tips?
fuck her way out by marrying some asshole?

        ginger's getting old
        fingertips gone from that artery shot
        veins calloused & collapsed

her drunken falls
fights she's had in jail
have streaked her face with scars

        other scars remind her she's an orphan
        & still grieving for her lover
        murdered by a cop-pusher

she can't concentrate very well

or even spell
but decides to say she's sick

            opens the bathroom door
            scraping against the floor
            like her soul screaming

she breathes deeply
builds a big phoney smile once more

            "I'm sorry honey" ginger says
            "but I can't make it right now
            I haven't been feeling too good lately
            tonight I just can't"

ginger's trick wants to know
"is it me? is that what you're trying to say?
did I do something?"

            'these bigshots think everything
            revolves around them
            little robot boys
            who at least come quick
            like striking a match
            blowing it out'

"no no no baby" ginger says
"it's not you
I like you
you're always so hot
it's just that I don't feel very good
but it's got nothing to do with you
I want to see you very soon okay?"

        the trick says
        "listen if it's something I've done
        to turn you off
        I don't know what the matter is"

ginger thinks
'at least he's getting dressed'

        "but I'm not going to pay for anything"
        he says

'a creep with a mansion
a wife guzzling scotch in the closet
kids screwing up in university'

        "oh no honey" ginger tells him
        "you don't have to pay
        there's something going around
        I must've caught it
        I'm really sorry
        we'll have a good time soon okay?

"there now baby
take care
see you
byyyeee"

■

when ginger walked into an alcoholic's anonymous meeting
wearing high heels & a tight low-cut dress
men rushed to help her

        ginger's prospects for a new way of life
        appeared to soar

        an older married man 25 years sober
        offered to take her under his wing
        reveal the spiritual essence of the
        program

he gave her a ride home
& put a heavy move on her
which ginger repulsed

        a spiked heel in the balls
        for the wound he opened in her heart

        ■

        "you're living off the avails of prostitution"
        ginger told me laughing

we'd talk about human change for days at a time

        I slept on her couch
        made runs for cheeseburgers &
        cigarettes
        from her penthouse apartment

a large framed portrait
of marilyn monroe on the wall

        & when the stockbrokers
        newspaper journalists
        chinatown gangsters
        came by to pay for it all

I'd wait in the lobby
& tell ginger how tough & cool they looked afterwards
she'd tell me how fragile they were before

                one night after an aa meeting
                at a skid row mission
                too broke to pay for a cab
                ginger said she'd risk it
                despite her terror of subways

we knew actual change
means descent
through a suffocating tunnel of fears

                I reassured her
                a late hour on a week night
                the cars would be empty

ginger punched the transfer machine 10 times
proof she rode
a subway train
at 10:32 on the 21st of june

                we're on the platform
                ginger's sweating
                I tell her everything will be all right

the train pulls into the station
hundreds of kids charge down the stairs
waving baseball pennants shouting yelling
jamming us into the car as the doors close

                ginger turns green
                sits down tight-lipped
                but manages to say
                "talk to me!"

I tell her it could be worse
we could be in new york
I imitate straphangers thrashed & flung
like dead beef
by screeching cars
lights flashing stroboscopically

                I'm jumping up & down in front of her
                jabbering & gesticulating

ginger starts laughing
& says
"I'll never trust you again!"

                she's already begun trusting
                SOMETHING
                infinitely wise

Hounded to the Coast

'We're on a hiiigggh-way to hell!' screams across the narrow aisle out of a ghetto blaster held by young jailbird tattoos.

Wild white boys piling into the rear seats.

'Sixty-nine hours to Vancouver,' the ticket seller had said.

Janice, a brand-new parolee, flops into the empty seat beside me. The judge exiled her from Toronto for two years, to Thunder Bay. Paroled to parents she hasn't seen in six years. She's drunk and showing off her slit-pocket booster-coat. Handing out valiums and passing a bottle of rum.

All I can think of is Marie, abandoned in a hell-hole hotel of drunken emergencies. But I was on the verge of jumping from the window there, or throwing someone else through it.

Silver comet splits the darkness, outside Sudbury.

A monstrous paper mill's blowing Bhopal-like clouds near Espanola. The hyper-anxious doctor's son who drank his way out of university, gets off at a blacked-out station, and heads for a bar before calling home.

Anthony, a passenger I meet at a rest stop, lets me know that Janice has told the old Frenchman who's been bugging her that I'm her pimp. I conjure grim scenarios . . . .

Anthony's a blues musician making his eighth trip to the coast in ten months. Says he doesn't know why, just knows he can't stop.

The woman in the seat ahead of me, who climbed aboard in

Sault Ste. Marie, says she's been in Toronto, and is going to Winnipeg to see her ex-husband, though her fiancé is waiting for her in Saskatoon. Somewhere along the way she ended up hitchhiking, a biker picked her up, gave her a ride and a ticket for this bus.

A girl from Costa Rica, an exchange student, fills a cup with water from the toilet tap, and appears startled and confused when a man warns her, 'Don't drink it, it's poison!' and a woman advises her, 'It's not really poison.'

The kid with the blaster and tattoos said he woke up drunk, rolled, and broke, in Buffalo. He lifts the white plaster cast covering his wrist and forearm more like a badge of honour than a flag of surrender.

Janice broadcasts a tabloid headline to the entire bus: 'Man solves his own murder!'

Another woman's reading a Pentecostal magazine. The man sitting next to her is reading **Hustler**.

Lake Superior, past Dead Horse Creek—trees... trees... trees... and glacial rock.

Bleak houses in battered White River, advertising itself as 'The Coldest Spot in Canada,' for hitting seventy-two below once upon a time.

Wild boys making noise and smoking. The driver pulls onto the highway shoulder, walks to the rear and tells them, 'There's not going to be any partying back here!' A wild boy blames Janice, 'She keeps tryin' to show us her boobs!' And Janice says, 'Hey, driver! They're just givin' you the grease!'

Through the window I see the 'World's Largest Oilcan' in Moosonin.

Amethyst Mines in Thunder Bay, Marie's astrological gem. A charm against drunkenness.

Old black and tan dog lying in the middle of a sunlit oil-stained bus bay. The nervous wide-blue-eyed novice missionary, who replaced Janice next to me, is on his way to a Native reserve. He stares at the dog and says, 'Boy, he isn't worried about anything, is he?'

In the station, a newspaper headline shouts: 'Cannibals Shrink Space Alien's Head!'

This is called a 'non-smoking fresh-air bus,' jam-packed and sour with stale sweat.

A new driver threatens, 'Don't smoke in the restroom, or I'll put you off the bus!' Smokers roll pop cans below the seats, rattling and clanging all the way to the driver's heels. Somebody yells, 'Let's put the driver off the bus!'

Lung-wracked coughing careens throughout the Greyhound, sounding like a mobile quarantine unit for some respiratory plague.

A pond with a large beaver lodge resting peacefully in it, beautiful with smooth sticks and mud . . .

A sign proclaims Niponee to be the home of Al Hackner, a curling champion.

The newest hound-boss admonishes the wild boys, 'I don't want you disturbing the other passengers!'

'They're disturbin' us!' a wild boy replies.

Riding in early grey afternoon . . .

'So you're the new driver,' a wild one says. 'Good, the last driver was drunk!'

A lengthy general discussion concerns cross-country welfare benefits. Which towns and cities let go of emergency cheques, or a meal, or an overnight flop.

A wild boy tells the conservatively dressed older man next to him, 'I trust you. You don't look like me. I know what I'm like.'

A black man reading a Reggie Jackson biography turns to a jabbering wild boy and says, 'You might notta been talkin' to me, but you mighta been talkin' about me!' And silences the boy with a hard stare.

Roadside rock like a petrified rainbow: blue, green, grey, white, black, yellow, red . . .

We stop at the Terry Fox Statue Lookout. A plaque reads: 'He left a challenge for each to meet in his own way.'

A very drunken man reels aboard, and soon reveals the contents of his travelling bag, nothing but Alcoholics Anonymous literature. He says he just got out of a treatment centre.

My thoughts turn to Marie, again and again. Watching the full moon fiery white in the clear sky, I imagine its light shining into her window too. And, as though it's a telepathic satellite, I bounce a prayer off the moon, expressing my hope for renewed love, to Marie.

On the restroom blackboard in Upsala, someone's written: 'Louie, your moose is tied up in Savant.'

Itinerant welders. Drywall workers. Tunnel labourers. Riding west, hoping for jobs. A fresh start...

At a rest stop, I opened a free copy of **Plain Truth** magazine, and learned that 'Greed is the underpinning of human nature.'

A small news sheet I picked up at a restaurant in the Soo reported that a seventeen-year-old female university student had been stabbed to death.

Twenty-five kilometres from Dryden, an inverted pentagram's painted on a boulder. A symbol for Satan...

Wild boys even louder, and nastier. Completely broke now, living on water and crackers.

It's Credit Union Day in Dryden. An enigmatic sign commands: 'Share the Vision.'

A cold-hearted white moon hangs over Kenora's Native miseries.

The wild boys were evicted as soon as we entered Manitoba. Furious, full of grievances, they threatened the driver, cursed Greyhound, and were left standing in a parking lot, impotently shaking their fists.

Morning sunlight flashes off Little Steel River. Short-ride Indians sit silently.

The young missionary from Pennsylvania's reading a paperback entitled **Witch Doctors and Sorcery**. One brief tale I skim involves a priest the Indians disliked enough to put a curse on him, so that whenever he tried to preach to them, he lost the ability to speak.

Before disembarking, the blond missionary was chewing his fingers and staring grimly at the road ahead.

Mostly poor people ride this bus that stops at expensive restaurants. An order of toast between two children. An orange between two hungry adults. Other passengers wait until diners have left their tables, then scoop the leftovers.

Stark sub-zero silvered pine tree in bone-blown Manitoba. Lone raven on a bare branch...

The ex-Vietnam vet behind me told his seatmate, a kindly looking elderly woman reading a Bible, that he just got out of a hospital. She asked what was wrong with him. He said, 'I thought the devil was chasing me. My psychiatrist told me a lot of people think that.'

I sink, self-pityingly, into my seat, like the stone sinking into my gut then pray Marie and I will be together soon—but saner, sober, and aware that we may not be on earth solely to make each other's lives sheer hell.

She and I detonate the deepest terrors in each other, unheal the oldest wounds. Being with each other is often like treading a minefield planted with bombs of trauma. Marie's family remained together no matter what violence they wrought upon each other. My family fled separately after each new explosion of rage and madness.

Marie and I grew up with murderers, suicides, alcoholics, drug addicts, thieves, convicts, mental patients, and rapists.

I remember my grandmother's summarizing statement,

when told a distant relative was compiling a genealogy: 'Why'd he want to do that? The ones we know about's bad enough!'
    Oh dear God, help Marie and me overcome ourselves.

Approaching Winnipeg, I see the Place Louis Riel spelled out in letters of fire and recall the Walt Whitman Hotel in degraded downtown Camden, New Jersey. Two poet-prophets of North America—exclusive hotels.

Night of insomniac hell, switching buses, and beside me a guy sleeping like he's digging a puck out of a corner. Elbows flailing.

Red-orange sunrise near Regina. Volcanic sky-island surfacing from snow-fields. Light-blue fog. Pale lavender horizon.

Another ten-minute rest stop. Anthony says he feels 'ridiculous,' forty-two years old, riding a Greyhound back and forth across the country, with a copy of Kerouac in his back pocket.

I tell Anthony my terrible blues with Marie. 'Maybe you really love her,' he says. 'I do!' I tell him passionately. Our five years together reeling kaleidoscopically through my mind.
    Five years of depressions, trances, addictions, starvations, mangled surgeries, desperation, tears and blood bursting from both of us—feeling doomed; but also joyous laughter, and intimacy such as only survivors from the worst of tragedies can feel, and our acts of selfless love, sometimes even recognized as such by the other.

An older woman in front of me explains to her seatmate her

reason for riding Greyhound: "My husband's almost totally deaf. So you don't talk unless you absolutely have to. And when you just sit around and look at the walls, and watch TV and read, I said, I'm going to Vancouver to stay with my son for a while."

Anthony says he's been through the rock-pop Holiday Inn studio-trip, and just wants to play the blues now. As soon as he can get off the highway.

  He knows individual waitresses by now in these bus stop diners, and whether to trust a meal, or just order soup.

  In Regina, he had an epiphany, declaring unequivocally that our waitress had 'the world's plainest brown dress.'

Riding another long night through, awake and aching, with lives thrown like dice down the highway . . .

In Tompkins, Saskatchewan, half-a-dozen ranchers board with their wives. Beginning a hound tour like they did ten years ago, to Las Vegas, San Diego, and Tijuana.

  'Three weeks in all. You only live once,' said the tall rancher beside me, with large sun-darkened hands, bulging forearms, a brown leisure suit with small Canadian flag lapel pin, cowboy boots, and a white Stetson hat.

  'A strange thing happened this year,' he said. 'It rained all of September. Half the grain rotted.' He couldn't recall that ever happening before.

  He said it was a good summer for him, but, 'There were a lot of closures for anyone started a farm or ranch in the last ten or fifteen years. They don't have a chance,' he said, softly, looking down at his hands, his face squeezed with compassion for men like those we see hanging out in prairie bus stations.

Hostile and curious looks from men in their thirties and forties 'who don't have a chance...'

A stop near Outlook, and I imagine the fierce blue-gold sky-wind roaring across the vast land blowing chains from my spirit and senses.

The old rancher keeps a diary. Spying over his shoulder, I read last night's entry: 'Rough night. Kept moving. Turning.'

Anthony complains about contemporary music, that it has become as colourless and moulded as 'ice cubes in a plastic tray.'

'Change the way we pray' is the last entry I read in the rancher's diary.

In Swift Current, a good-natured Italian tourist camera bug who's been stalking the aisle for photo opportunities, lugging all manner of camera paraphernalia, shooting out of the window, was attacked by an old man in the first seat by the door. He apparently thought the Italian was taking a picture of him, and drilled the camera lens with a right hook, but failed to knock out the exuberance of the Italian, who has provided comic relief, trapping himself in the Greyhound crapper, and struggling with the door for several minutes before extricating himself, red-faced and grinning, to be greeted by laughter and applause from the rest of us.

Someone surmised the old man became so offended by the camera because he was probably in the Witness Protection Program. I thought perhaps the old man subscribed to the belief that the artificial reproductive capabilities of the camera diminishes the spirit, or steals the soul of the person photographed. Most likely, the extrovert Italian just got on his nerves.

The Italian chose this Greyhound route specifically so he could take photos of the Rocky Mountains, but was rendered speechless when informed we'd be passing through the mountains in the dead of night.

Reflection of a tree, dark-blue, floats amidst mountain shadows, in the middle of a pond, in Alberta.

Now that the Italian has recovered from his shock about crossing the Rockies in darkness, he's photographing people in doughnut shops and restaurants.

A young guy in the seat beside me has been guzzling bottle after bottle of codeine-laced cough syrup. I recently read that Canadians consume more codeine per capita than people in any other industrialized country.

   I have certainly done my damnedest to help Canada reach the top in that category. Over-the-counter Tylenol with codeine just about killed me. I ended up taking lethal dosages to prevent withdrawal sickness from the codeine, and consequently overdosed on the Tylenol.

   In the emergency room, a nurse told me Tylenol overdoses were common. Two doctors appeared, looked at my test results on a clipboard, and gaped at me with open mouths. Then one of them blurted a question I've been asking myself for most of my life: 'Why are you still alive?'

   All I could do was hold up my hands.

Outside Medicine Hat, twenty years ago, were trailers with showers and bunks and hot food, provided free for road-weary travellers by the federal government. Today in Medicine Hat, it's twenty cents to take a shit, plus graffiti: 'Fuck You And Everyone That Looks Like You!'

Twenty years ago in Medicine Hat, a very old Indian woman walked past me on the sidewalk, stopped and turned to face me. She stood there looking into my soul, it felt like, and her eyes began pouring tears.

She walked slowly up to me, and when quite close, thrust a two-dollar bill into my hand, and said, 'My heart is sad for you.'

I stood there, astonished, as she walked away.

So many empty, abandoned houses throughout the forests and prairies, near small towns, on open land, with no way for anyone to live in them. People forced by economic techniques into urban pressure cookers.

Greyhound drivers drinking coffee in a restaurant, talking grievances filed, breakdown schedules endured...

Calgary's lights at night, spread alluringly like petals and tendrils of a bright carnivorous flower.

Horrific farting turning the hound-bus into a gas chamber.

I finally passed out, and woke up sweating.

'Emergency exit... Lift this bar... Push window open.'

I look around at my fellow passengers trying to sleep, wrestling with themselves in their seats. No contortionist performance artist I've ever seen has executed such excruciating postures as we do, trying to fit comfortably into these impossibly cramped seats.

I snatch a newspaper from the floor and read that a psychiatrist has announced the first conference to study and discuss: 'Self-mutilation... more common than you think... discovered like bulimics and multiple personalities... people ashamed to admit it... covered by clothing.'

No revelation to me. I've swallowed and inhaled poisons, stabbed needles into my veins, slashed razor blades across my arms, and purposely driven an automobile into a wall at sixty miles an hour.

I've known people who pour acid on themselves, eat broken glass, stick their fingers intentionally into light sockets, viciously bite themselves, shoot bullets into their feet and practice various other disfigurements—inflicting lacerations and burns—as though attempting to mortify some unspeakable, shameful experience. And yet I've heard of religious people who wear hair shirts, put sharp stones in their shoes, or wear belts with nails embedded in their flesh.

But then, the religious do that in order to be reminded of God. The rest of us do that to be reminded of ourselves.

A sign says: 'Mountains.' Wet rock beside the highway...

At Banff, young ski-resorters crowd the bus. I'm tired, anxious, stinking, and they seem to me prattling, puffed-up, pretentious, cream-filled beings who've never missed a meal in their lives. My judgmental attitude bugs me more than they do.

The communion between Marie and me, at the last moment, as I was leaving for the bus station, comes back to me as something miraculous.

No matter how frustrating trying to love and receive love

has been for us, we re-sealed a deep connection that drew us to each other in the first place.

Marie called me 'friend' more fervently—and with such a radiant expression—than I've ever received from anyone.

Then we embraced, outside hotel hell, where guardian angels hovered over us.

A banner at the Mohawk gas station in Golden says: 'Reward Yourself.' But it doesn't say for what.

Headline in a Yellowknife newspaper: 'Drunks disrupt assembly.' They'll do it every time.

Heavy rain falling...

'I'm Chinese, sorry, I don't speak English,' says a man in suit and tie, to a cowboy who replies, 'That's okay. A lot of people in Canada don't speak English.'

I smoke a cigarette in the rain at Hope, where **Rambo** was filmed. That movie's inspired a loner-army of camouflage-dressed psychotics, committing mayhem in neighbourhoods and on city streets throughout North America.

Should be some kind of victims' commemorative plaque, or at least a marker reading 'He left a challenge....'

Closing in on Vancouver. Crowded-bus-rush-hour-torture. Humpty-Dumpty, the businessman, is wedged beside me, squirming with boils on his ass, he tells me. My own spinal fractures are biting me with sharp teeth

I have come out here to die—like how many other Greyhound refugees, burning a continent behind them?

I've come here to die, either ignominiously in some wretched situation, or to my old life. But this is it. Nowhere left to run except into the ocean.

And Marie said she too would be riding the 'hound to Vancouver, to me, when she was ready....

Heljo, a friend of Marie's and mine, and the woman who paid my fare out here, was driven, terror-stricken, through bomb-wracked Europe during the Second World War. Heljo, from Estonia, was more than once buried alive with debris, shattered bricks, and scorched wood, but survived to build a new life in Canada. She told me she believes Marie and I will rise like 'mated phoenixes.'

Hounded to the coast, by furies and angels...

Hounded to the coast, to annihilation or resurrection...

Lunar eclipse. Skyline. Green dawn.